The NO-STRESS HOLIDAY ORGANIZER

The NO-STRESS HOLIDAY ORGANIZER

AN ALL-IN-ONE GUIDE TO PLANNING AND RECORDING YOUR HOLIDAYS

PLAIN SIGHT PUBLISHING
AN IMPRINT OF CEDAR FORT, INC.
SPRINGVILLE, UTAH

ISBN 13: 978-1-4621-1491-7

Published by Plain Sight Publishing, an imprint of Cedar Fort, Inc.
2373 W. 700 S., Springville, UT 84663
Distributed by Cedar Fort, Inc., www.cedarfort.com

LIBRARY OF CONGRESS CATALOGING-IN-PUBLICATION DATA

Lindsley, Whitney, 1987-author.
 The No-stress holiday organizer / Whitney Lindsley.
    pages cm
 ISBN 978-1-4621-1491-7 (alk. paper)
 1. Holidays. 2. Entertaining. 3. Parties--Planning. I. Title.

 GT4803.A2L56 2014
 394.26--dc23
                                             2014018264

Cover and page design by Angela D. Baxter
Cover design © 2014 by Lyle Mortimer
Edited by Daniel Friend

Printed in the United States of America

10 9 8 7 6 5 4 3 2 1

Printed on acid-free paper

HAPPY HOLIDAYS!

ARE YOU READY FOR ALL YOUR PARTIES, DINNERS, AND OTHER FESTIVITIES? IF YOU ANSWERED NO, THEN *THE NO-STRESS HOLIDAY ORGANIZER* IS HERE TO HELP! NOT ONLY DOES IT INCLUDE CALENDARS AND TO-DO LISTS, BUT IT ALSO INCLUDES RECIPES, BUDGET SHEETS, AND GROCERY LISTS TO HELP YOU GET YOUR ACT TOGETHER THIS HOLIDAY SEASON. THIS PLANNER IS BROKEN UP BY HOLIDAY—THANKSGIVING, CHRISTMAS, AND NEW YEAR'S—WITH PAGES TAILORED TO THOSE SPECIAL DAYS. YOUR HOLIDAY SEASON IS SURE TO BE GREAT AS YOU FOLLOW THE TIPS AND TRICKS IN THIS PLANNER.

FOR THE YEAR

CONTENTS

NOVEMBER

1

DECEMBER

43

JANUARY

THREE-MONTH
AT-A-GLANCE CALENDAR

FILL IN THE DATES TO MATCH THE CURRENT YEAR, THEN USE THESE
CALENDARS TO GET AN OVERVIEW OF THIS HOLIDAY SEASON.

NOVEMBER

SUNDAY	MONDAY	TUESDAY	WEDNESDAY	THURSDAY	FRIDAY	SATURDAY

DECEMBER

SUNDAY	MONDAY	TUESDAY	WEDNESDAY	THURSDAY	FRIDAY	SATURDAY

JANUARY

SUNDAY	MONDAY	TUESDAY	WEDNESDAY	THURSDAY	FRIDAY	SATURDAY

NOVEMBER

FOR EACH NEW MORNING WITH ITS LIGHT,
FOR REST AND SHELTER OF THE NIGHT,
FOR HEALTH AND FOOD,
FOR LOVE AND FRIENDS,
FOR EVERYTHING THY GOODNESS SENDS.

—RALPH WALDO EMERSON

1

NOVEMBER

SUNDAY	MONDAY	TUESDAY

WEDNESDAY	THURSDAY	FRIDAY	SATURDAY

Simply
THANKFUL

· ·

TO-DO LIST

JOT DOWN ALL THE THINGS YOU NEED TO DO TO GET READY
FOR THANKSGIVING AND CHECK THEM OFF AS YOU GO!

☐ _____   ☐ _____

☐ _____   ☐ _____

☐ _____   ☐ _____

☐ _____   ☐ _____

☐ _____   ☐ _____

☐ _____   ☐ _____

☐ _____   ☐ _____

☐ _____   ☐ _____

☐ _____   ☐ _____

☐ _____   ☐ _____

☐ _____   ☐ _____

☐ _____   ☐ _____

☐ _____   ☐ _____

THANKSGIVING BUDGET

PLAN AHEAD FOR ALL YOUR THANKSGIVING EXPENSES

	ESTIMATED	ACTUAL
GREETINGS	$	$
PHOTOS		
CARDS		
ENVELOPES		
POSTAGE		
INVITATIONS		
DECOR	$	$
INDOOR DECORATIONS		
OUTDOOR DECORATIONS		
SUPPLIES		
CRAFT SUPPLIES		
OTHER		
OTHER		

	ESTIMATED	ACTUAL
FOOD	$	$
HOLIDAY MEALS		
PARTIES		
BAKING		
EATING OUT		
DRINKS		
OTHER		
TRAVEL	$	$
TRANSPORTATION		
LODGING		
OTHER		
MISCELLANEOUS	$	$
CLOTHING		
TICKETS		
TOTALS	$	$

THANKSGIVING DECORATIONS

KEEP TRACK OF ALL YOUR THANKSGIVING DECORATION IDEAS

DECORATION	HAVE	NEED	WHERE TO BUY/BORROW

SUPPLIES	HAVE	NEED	WHERE TO BUY/BORROW

We gather
TOGETHER

GUEST LIST & CONTACT INFO

NAME _____ PHONE NUMBER _____ RSVP ATTENDING?
ADDRESS _____ EMAIL ADDRESS _____ ☐   ☐

NAME _____ PHONE NUMBER _____ RSVP ATTENDING?
ADDRESS _____ EMAIL ADDRESS _____ ☐   ☐

NAME _____ PHONE NUMBER _____ RSVP ATTENDING?
ADDRESS _____ EMAIL ADDRESS _____ ☐   ☐

NAME _____ PHONE NUMBER _____ RSVP ATTENDING?
ADDRESS _____ EMAIL ADDRESS _____ ☐   ☐

NAME _____ PHONE NUMBER _____ RSVP ATTENDING?
ADDRESS _____ EMAIL ADDRESS _____ ☐   ☐

NAME _____ PHONE NUMBER _____ RSVP ATTENDING?
ADDRESS _____ EMAIL ADDRESS _____ ☐   ☐

NAME _____ PHONE NUMBER _____ RSVP ATTENDING?
ADDRESS _____ EMAIL ADDRESS _____ ☐   ☐

NAME _____ PHONE NUMBER _____ RSVP ATTENDING?
ADDRESS _____ EMAIL ADDRESS _____ ☐   ☐

NAME _____ PHONE NUMBER _____ RSVP ATTENDING?
ADDRESS _____ EMAIL ADDRESS _____ ☐   ☐

NAME _____ PHONE NUMBER _____ RSVP ATTENDING?
ADDRESS _____ EMAIL ADDRESS _____ ☐   ☐

NAME _____ PHONE NUMBER _____ RSVP ATTENDING?
ADDRESS _____ EMAIL ADDRESS _____ ☐   ☐

NAME _____ PHONE NUMBER _____ RSVP ATTENDING?
ADDRESS _____ EMAIL ADDRESS _____ ☐   ☐

NAME _____ PHONE NUMBER _____ RSVP ATTENDING?
ADDRESS _____ EMAIL ADDRESS _____ ☐   ☐

NAME _____ PHONE NUMBER _____ RSVP ATTENDING?
ADDRESS _____ EMAIL ADDRESS _____ ☐   ☐

THANKSGIVING

PARTY PLANNING COUNTDOWN

WHETHER IT'S A SMALL MEAL OR A LARGE AFFAIR, DON'T FORGET THE DETAILS!

3-4 WEEKS BEFORE

- [ ] PLAN THE MENU
- [ ] CREATE GROCERY LIST
- [ ] CREATE GUEST LIST
- [ ] DISPENSE FOOD ASSIGNMENTS
- [ ] DESIGN INVITATIONS (OPTIONAL)
- [ ] INVENTORY COOKING EQUIPMENT
- [ ] ARRANGE TO BORROW ANY NEEDED SUPPLIES
- [ ] PLAN DECORATIONS (TABLE, HOME, AND SO ON)
- [ ] BUY ANY NECESSARY DECORATIONS
- [ ] DECORATE NOW OR A LITTLE LATER

2 WEEKS BEFORE

- [ ] MAP OUT THE BEST PLACES TO BUY FOOD
- [ ] CLIP COUPONS AND COMPARE PRICES
- [ ] BUY THE TURKEY AND NONPERISHABLE FOOD TO AVOID THE RUSH
- [ ] BUY DECORATIONS
- [ ] SEND OUT INVITATIONS IF NECESSARY
- [ ] CONFIRM FOOD ASSIGNMENTS WITH FAMILY

1 WEEK BEFORE

- [ ] GATHER ENOUGH TABLES AND CHAIRS
- [ ] BEGIN CLEANING THE HOUSE (START WITH LOWER-TRAFFIC AREAS)
- [ ] BUY ANY NEEDED BULK ITEMS (SUCH AS PAPER PLATES, PLASTIC WARE, AND SO ON)
- [ ] CONFIRM WITH GUESTS THAT THEY'RE ATTENDING

- [ ] TRY OUT ANY NEW RECIPES TO MAKE SURE YOU WANT TO SERVE THEM
- [ ] GATHER TABLECLOTHS IF NEEDED

WEEK OF

- [ ] BUY PERISHABLE FOOD ITEMS
- [ ] CONFIRM WITH ANY GUESTS WHO HAVEN'T RESPONDED TO THE INVITATION
- [ ] DOUBLE-CHECK FOOD ASSIGNMENTS
- [ ] CLEAN HIGHER-TRAFFIC AREAS (BATHROOMS, BEDROOMS, LIVING ROOM, KITCHEN)
- [ ] BRINE TURKEY IF NECESSARY
- [ ] GATHER SERVING DISHES, SILVERWARE, AND SO ON
- [ ] WASH THE LINENS

DAY BEFORE

- [ ] MAKE THE PIES
- [ ] PREPARE ANY MAKE-AHEAD RECIPES
- [ ] CLEAN ANY REMAINING AREAS/ROOMS
- [ ] VACUUM
- [ ] PUT ANY FINISHING TOUCHES ON THE TABLE DECORATIONS

DAY OF

- [ ] SET THE TABLE
- [ ] PUT THE TURKEY IN THE OVEN ON TIME
- [ ] COOK ANY DISHES ASSIGNED TO YOU— DON'T FORGET THOSE EXTRAS
- [ ] WELCOME GUESTS
- [ ] ENJOY YOUR MEAL!

PARTY PLANNING

PARTY DATE: _____ PARTY BEGINS: _____ PARTY ENDS: _____

PARTY THEME: _____

PARTY STYLE: _____

THEME IDEAS

- GRATITUDE—PROVIDE NOTE CARDS SO YOUR GUESTS CAN WRITE DOWN THINGS THEY'RE GRATEFUL FOR AND HAVE THEM TAKE TURNS READING THEM ALOUD.

- GIVING BACK—ASK GUESTS TO BRING A CAN OF FOOD TO DONATE TO YOUR LOCAL FOOD BANK.

- AUTUMN HARVEST—DECORATE WITH NATURAL ELEMENTS LIKE PUMPKINS, BRANCHES, PINE CONES, AND FALL LEAVES IN RED, ORANGE, AND YELLOW.

ACTIVITIES

_____

_____

_____

_____

_____

 TIP EMAILED INVITATIONS WORK JUST AS WELL AS TRADITIONAL INVITATIONS. HOWEVER, TRADITIONAL INVITATIONS MORE FORMAL AND PERSONAL.

Bless all who

GATHER HERE

· ·

THANKSGIVING MENU PLAN

WHAT'S ON THE MENU? PLANNING IT OUT IN ADVANCE WILL HELP YOU KEEP TRACK OF
ALL THE DELICIOUS THINGS THAT WILL BE PART OF YOUR HOLIDAY CELEBRATION!

MEAL LOCATION: _____

TIME AND DATE: _____

	COURSE/MENU ITEM	RECIPE SOURCE	WHO'S MAKING IT?
APPETIZER			
APPETIZER			
APPETIZER			
APPETIZER			
SALAD			
BREAD			
ENTREE			
ENTREE			
MAIN DISH			
MAIN DISH			
SIDE DISH			
SIDE DISH			
DESSERT			
DESSERT			
BEVERAGES			
OTHER			
OTHER			
OTHER			
OTHER			

TIP CHECK WITH YOUR GUESTS TO SEE IF THERE ARE ANY
FOOD ALLERGIES OR DIETARY RESTRICTIONS YOU SHOULD
BE AWARE OF WHEN PLANNING YOUR MEAL.

THINGS TO MAKE & THINGS TO BUY

NOT EVERYTHING NEEDS TO BE HOMEMADE TO MAKE A MEMORABLE THANKSGIVING DINNER. TAKE SOME OF THE STRESS OFF AND USE SOME THINGS PREMADE FROM THE STORE. KEEP TRACK OF WHAT THINGS YOU'LL BE COOKING AND WHAT THINGS YOU'LL BE BUYING.

THINGS TO MAKE	THINGS TO BUY

TIP IF THERE WILL BE YOUNGER KIDS AT YOUR THANKSGIVING FEAST, MAKE SURE THERE ARE PLENTY OF KID-FRIENDLY FOODS AVAILABLE AND A KIDS' TABLE SET UP JUST FOR THEM.

GROCERY LIST

MAKE A LIST OF EVERYTHING YOU'LL NEED SO YOU WON'T HAVE TO MAKE ANY LAST-MINUTE TRIPS TO THE STORE.

PRODUCE
- ☐ _____
- ☐ _____
- ☐ _____
- ☐ _____
- ☐ _____
- ☐ _____

MEAT/POULTRY
- ☐ _____
- ☐ _____
- ☐ _____
- ☐ _____
- ☐ _____
- ☐ _____

DELI/BAKERY
- ☐ _____
- ☐ _____
- ☐ _____
- ☐ _____
- ☐ _____
- ☐ _____

CANNED GOODS
- ☐ _____
- ☐ _____
- ☐ _____
- ☐ _____
- ☐ _____
- ☐ _____

DRY GOODS
- ☐ _____
- ☐ _____
- ☐ _____
- ☐ _____
- ☐ _____
- ☐ _____

BAKING ITEMS/SPICES
- ☐ _____
- ☐ _____
- ☐ _____
- ☐ _____
- ☐ _____
- ☐ _____

CONDIMENTS
- ☐ _____
- ☐ _____
- ☐ _____
- ☐ _____
- ☐ _____
- ☐ _____

SNACKS
- ☐ _____
- ☐ _____
- ☐ _____
- ☐ _____
- ☐ _____
- ☐ _____

DAIRY
- ☐ _____
- ☐ _____
- ☐ _____
- ☐ _____
- ☐ _____
- ☐ _____

DRINKS
- ☐ _____
- ☐ _____
- ☐ _____
- ☐ _____
- ☐ _____
- ☐ _____

FROZEN
- ☐ _____
- ☐ _____
- ☐ _____
- ☐ _____
- ☐ _____
- ☐ _____

MISCELLANEOUS
- ☐ _____
- ☐ _____
- ☐ _____
- ☐ _____
- ☐ _____
- ☐ _____

COOKING SCHEDULE

PLANNING A FULL THANKSGIVING MEAL CAN FEEL LIKE AN OVERWHELMING TASK, BUT SCHEDULING YOUR MENU AND KEEPING TRACK OF ALL THE STEPS THAT NEED TO BE DONE WILL TAKE AWAY THE STRESS AND HELP YOU PREPARE A PERFECT MEAL.

DISH	WEEK OF	DAY BEFORE	DAY OF	COOKING METHOD	COOKING/SERVING DISH	PREP TIME	BAKING/ COOKING TIME	COOKING TEMP

DAY BEFORE

6 AM					
7 AM					
8 AM					
9 AM					
10 AM					
11 AM					
12 PM					
1 PM					
2 PM					
3 PM					
4 PM					
5 PM					
6 PM					
7 PM					

DAY OF

6 AM					
7 AM					
8 AM					
9 AM					
10 AM					
11 AM					
12 PM					
1 PM					
2 PM					
3 PM					
4 PM					
5 PM					
6 PM					
7 PM					

PREP LIST ORDER

PREPARING YOUR
THANKSGIVING TURKEY

 TIP

HOW TO THAW A TURKEY
FROZEN WHOLE TURKEYS AND FROZEN WHOLE TURKEY BREASTS NEED TO BE THAWED BEFORE COOKING. FOR THE BEST RESULTS, FOLLOW ONE OF THESE METHODS:

REFRIGERATOR THAWING
THAW UNOPENED, BREAST SIDE UP, ON A TRAY IN THE FRIDGE.

ALLOW AT LEAST 1 DAY OF THAWING FOR EVERY 4 LBS.

COLD-WATER THAWING

THAW UNOPENED, BREAST SIDE DOWN, WITH ENOUGH COLD WATER TO COVER YOUR TURKEY COMPLETELY.

CHANGE THE WATER EVERY 30 MINUTES TO KEEP THE TURKEY CHILLED.

ESTIMATE A MINIMUM THAWING TIME OF 30 MINUTES PER LB.

A THAWED TURKEY MAY BE KEPT IN THE REFRIGERATOR FOR UP TO 4 DAYS BEFORE COOKING.

SOURCE: WWW.BUTTERBALL.COM/HOW-TOS/THAW-A-TURKEY

TIP

HOW TO CARVE A TURKEY
CARVING ALWAYS BEGINS WITH THE UTENSILS. USE A SHARPENED, STRAIGHT-EDGE KNIFE AND A CARVING FORK TO CARVE YOUR TURKEY.

CARVING THE BREAST
FIRST, ALLOW YOUR COOKED TURKEY TO SIT FOR ABOUT 20 MINUTES BEFORE STARTING TO CARVE.

BEGINNING HALFWAY UP THE BREAST, SLICE STRAIGHT DOWN WITH AN EVEN STROKE.

WHEN THE KNIFE REACHES THE CUT ABOVE THE WING JOINT, THE SLICE SHOULD FALL FREE ON ITS OWN.

CONTINUE TO SLICE BREAST MEAT BY STARTING THE CUT AT A HIGHER POINT EACH TIME.

DRUMSTICKS
CUT THE BAND OF SKIN HOLDING THE DRUMSTICKS.

GRASP THE END OF THE DRUMSTICK. PLACE YOUR KNIFE BETWEEN THE DRUMSTICK AND THIGH AND THE BODY OF THE TURKEY, AND CUT THROUGH THE SKIN TO THE JOINT.

REMOVE THE ENTIRE LEG BY PULLING OUT AND BACK, USING THE POINT OF THE KNIFE TO SEPARATE THE JOINT.

SEPARATE THE THIGH AND DRUMSTICK AT THE JOINT.

WINGS
INSERT CARVING FORK IN THE UPPER WING TO STEADY THE TURKEY.

MAKE A LONG HORIZONTAL CUT ABOVE THE WING JOINT THROUGH THE BODY FRAME.

THE WING CAN BE REMOVED FROM THE BODY IF DESIRED.

SOURCE: WWW.BUTTERBALL.COM/HOW-TOS/CARVE-A-TURKEY

RECIPES

HERE ARE A FEW RECIPES TO HELP YOU CREATE A DELICIOUS THANKSGIVING FEAST!

THANKSGIVING TURKEY

1 (12-lb.) Whole turkey, thawed
¾ cup butter, divided and cubed

1 (1-oz.) pkg. Italian dressing mix
2 cups water

1. Preheat oven to 325 degrees F (165 degrees C). Clean turkey (discard giblets and organs) and place in a roasting pan with a lid.

2. Using a sharp knife, poke holes in the skin of the turkey. Rub ½ package Italian dressing mix under the skin of the turkey. Insert ¼ cup cubed butter into holes made previously. Melt remaining ½ cup butter in microwave set on low. Combine remaining ½ package Italian dressing mix with melted butter.

3. Using a basting brush, apply the butter mixture to the outside of the uncooked turkey. Pour water into the bottom of the roasting pan and cover.

3. Bake turkey for 3 hours. Uncover and bake for an additional hour or until the internal temperature of the thickest part of the thigh measures 180 degrees F (82 degrees C). Remove bird from oven and allow to rest for about 30 minutes before carving.

THANKSGIVING STUFFING

1½ cups boiling water
¾ cup butter
½ cup onion, chopped
¼ tsp. pepper
1 Tbsp. powdered sage
1½ tsp. salt

½ Tbsp. dry mustard (optional)
2 Tbsp. celery, diced
1 loaf of bread, cubed and
   dried for one day
1½ Tbsp. parsley flakes
turkey giblets (optional)

1. Combine all ingredients in a pan except for the bread. If using turkey giblets, cook until giblets are done.

2. Remove giblets and dice into small pieces.

3. Add back into the mixture and spoon over the bread so it is moist but not soggy. This recipe should make enough to stuff an 8-lb. turkey.

MAKE-AHEAD MASHED POTATOES

1 Tbsp. salt
9 potatoes, peeled and cubed
6 oz. cream cheese, softened
1 cup sour cream (or plain yogurt)

2 tsp. seasoning salt, heaping
1 tsp. garlic powder
¼ tsp. ground black pepper
2 Tbsp. butter

1. Bring a large pot of salted water to a boil. Drop in potatoes and cook until tender but still firm, about 15 minutes.

2. Transfer potatoes to a large bowl and mash until smooth. Mix in the cream cheese, sour cream, onion powder, salt, pepper, and butter. Cover and refrigerate 8 hours or overnight.

3. Preheat oven to 350 degrees F (175 degrees C). Lightly grease a medium baking dish. Spread potato mixture into the prepared baking dish and bake about 30 minutes.

TIP: This recipe can be reheated in a Crock-Pot. Transfer potatoes to Crock-Pot the morning of the meal and let heat for 8 hours on low.

PUMPKIN PIE

3 eggs
1 cup sugar
½ tsp. salt
1 tsp. cinnamon
½ tsp. nutmeg

¼ tsp. cloves
1½ cups milk
1½ cups pumpkin
1 unbaked pie crust

1. Beat eggs slightly. Add sugar, salt, and spices and stir well.

2. Add milk gradually, add pumpkin, and mix thoroughly.

3. Pour in an unbaked pie crust and bake at 450 degrees F (230 degrees C) for 15 minutes. Reduce heat to 350 degrees F (177 degrees C) and bake 40 minutes more.

NOW IT'S YOUR TURN! WRITE DOWN YOUR TRADITIONAL
THANKSGIVING RECIPES FOR EASY ACCESS.

In everything,
GIVE THANKS

TRADITIONS

TAKE TIME TO REFLECT ON SOME OF YOUR FAVORITE
THANKSGIVING DAY FAMILY TRADITIONS.

TRADITION: _____

_____

_____

_____

_____

_____

TRADITION: _____

_____

_____

_____

_____

_____

TRADITION: _____

_____

_____

_____

_____

_____

DO YOU HAVE ANY THANKSGIVING TRADITIONS THAT ARE UNIQUE TO YOUR FAMILY?

TRADITION: _____

_____

_____

_____

_____

_____

TRADITION: _____

_____

_____

_____

_____

_____

TRADITION: _____

_____

_____

_____

_____

_____

WHAT TRADITIONS WOULD YOU LIKE TO START NEXT THANKSGIVING?

NEW TRADITION:_____

_____

_____

_____

_____

_____

NEW TRADITION:_____

_____

_____

_____

_____

_____

NEW TRADITION:_____

_____

_____

_____

_____

_____

Take time
TO BE THANKFUL

REFLECTIONS

WHAT ARE SOME OF YOUR FAVORITE THANKSGIVING
MEMORIES THIS YEAR?

MEMORY: _____

_____

_____

_____

_____

MEMORY: _____

_____

_____

_____

_____

_____

MEMORY: _____

_____

_____

_____

_____

_____

WHAT WAS YOUR FAVORITE THING ABOUT THIS THANKSGIVING?

WHAT WAS THE BEST PART OF YOUR THANKSGIVING DINNER?

WHAT FAMILY AND FRIENDS DID YOU GET TO SPEND TIME WITH OR KEEP IN TOUCH WITH THIS THANKSGIVING?

WHAT DO YOU LOOK FORWARD TO NEXT THANKSGIVING?

USE THE SPACE BELOW FOR ANY OTHER THOUGHTS OR MEMORIES.

Count your
BLESSINGS

GRATITUDE LIST

WHAT ARE SOME OF THE THINGS YOU ARE MOST GRATEFUL FOR?

{ PHOTO }

{PHOTO}

{PHOTO}

{PHOTO}

{PHOTO}

{ PHOTO }

Give
THANKS

BLACK FRIDAY SHOPPING LIST

READY TO SHOP TILL YOU DROP? PLAN YOUR ROUTE AND YOUR
STRATEGY BEFORE YOU GO SO YOU CAN SCORE SOME KILLER DEALS!

PRIORITY **STORE** _____
☐ WEBSITE _____

STORE OPENS/SALE BEGINS [____]

PRICE

SPECIAL DEALS
_____ _____
_____ _____
_____ _____
_____ _____
_____ _____

PRIORITY **STORE** _____
☐ WEBSITE _____

STORE OPENS/SALE BEGINS [____]

PRICE

SPECIAL DEALS
_____ _____
_____ _____
_____ _____
_____ _____
_____ _____

PRIORITY **STORE** _____
☐ WEBSITE _____

STORE OPENS/SALE BEGINS [____]

PRICE

SPECIAL DEALS
_____ _____
_____ _____
_____ _____
_____ _____
_____ _____

PRIORITY **STORE** _____
☐ WEBSITE _____

STORE OPENS/SALE BEGINS [____]

PRICE

SPECIAL DEALS
_____ _____
_____ _____
_____ _____
_____ _____
_____ _____

PRIORITY **STORE** _____
☐ WEBSITE _____

STORE OPENS/SALE BEGINS [____]

PRICE

SPECIAL DEALS
_____ _____
_____ _____
_____ _____
_____ _____
_____ _____

PRIORITY **STORE** _____
☐ WEBSITE _____

STORE OPENS/SALE BEGINS [____]

PRICE

SPECIAL DEALS
_____ _____
_____ _____
_____ _____
_____ _____
_____ _____

TIP GET AN EARLY START AND HIT THE STORES IN ORDER OF PRIORITY.
REMEMBER, BE SAFE AND KEEP YOUR COMMON SENSE—NO NEW SWEATER
OR ELECTRONIC GADGET IS WORTH GETTING A BLACK EYE!

DECEMBER

"THERE SEEMS A MAGIC IN THE
VERY NAME OF CHRISTMAS."
—CHARLES DICKENS

DECEMBER

SUNDAY	MONDAY	TUESDAY
4	5	6
11	12	13
18	19	20
25	26	27

WEDNESDAY	THURSDAY	FRIDAY	SATURDAY
	1	2	3
7	8	9	10
14	15	16	17
21	22	23	24
28	29	30	31

'Tis the
SEASON

TO-DO LIST

JOT DOWN ALL THE THINGS YOU NEED TO DO TO GET READY
FOR CHRISTMAS AND CHECK THEM OFF AS YOU GO!

- [ ] _____
- [ ] _____
- [ ] _____
- [ ] _____
- [ ] _____
- [ ] _____
- [ ] _____
- [ ] _____
- [ ] _____
- [ ] _____
- [ ] _____
- [ ] _____
- [ ] _____

- [ ] _____
- [ ] _____
- [ ] _____
- [ ] _____
- [ ] _____
- [ ] _____
- [ ] _____
- [ ] _____
- [ ] _____
- [ ] _____
- [ ] _____
- [ ] _____
- [ ] _____

CHRISTMAS BUDGET

PLAN AHEAD FOR ALL YOUR CHRISTMAS EXPENSES

GIFTS	ESTIMATED $	ACTUAL $
SPOUSE/SIGNIFICANT OTHER		
KIDS		
PARENTS		
SIBLINGS		
NIECES/NEPHEWS		
GRANDPARENTS		
OTHER RELATIVES		
FRIENDS		
NEIGHBORS		
COWORKERS		
HOSTESS GIFTS		
TEACHERS		
STOCKING STUFFERS		
GIFT WRAP AND TAGS		
SHIPPING		
CHARITABLE GIFTS/DONATIONS		
OTHER		

GREETINGS	$	$
PHOTOS		
CARDS		
ENVELOPES		
POSTAGE		
INVITATIONS		

DECOR	$	$
TREE		
LIGHTS		
ORNAMENTS		
INDOOR DECORATIONS		
OUTDOOR DECORATIONS		
SUPPLIES		
CRAFT SUPPLIES		
OTHER		

FOOD	ESTIMATED $	ACTUAL $
HOLIDAY MEALS		
PARTIES		
BAKING		
EATING OUT		
DRINKS		
OTHER		

TRAVEL	$	$
TRANSPORTATION		
LODGING		
OTHER		

MISCELLANEOUS	$	$
CLOTHING		
TICKETS		

TOTALS	$	$

CHRISTMAS DECORATIONS

KEEP TRACK OF ALL YOUR CHRISTMAS DECORATION IDEAS

DECORATION	HAVE	NEED	WHERE TO BUY/BORROW

SUPPLIES	HAVE	NEED	WHERE TO BUY/BORROW

CHRISTMAS WISH LISTS

MAKE A LIST FOR CLOSE FRIENDS AND FAMILY
SO YOU'LL GET THEM SOMETHING THEY'LL LOVE!

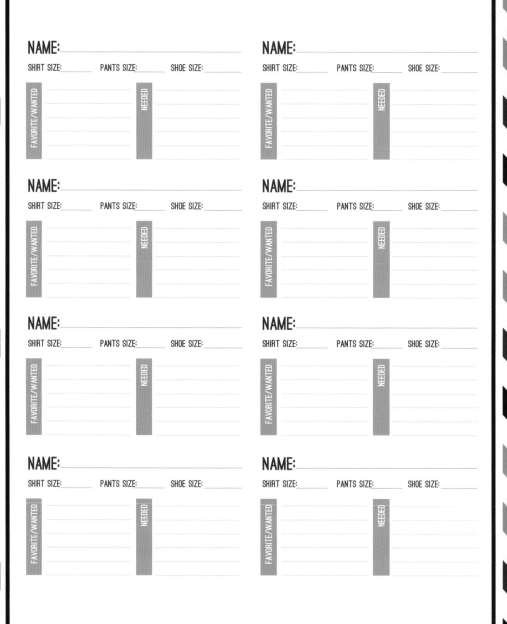

NAME:

SHIRT SIZE: _____ PANTS SIZE: _____ SHOE SIZE: _____

FAVORITE/WANTED   NEEDED

NAME:

SHIRT SIZE: _____ PANTS SIZE: _____ SHOE SIZE: _____

FAVORITE/WANTED   NEEDED

NAME:

SHIRT SIZE: _____ PANTS SIZE: _____ SHOE SIZE: _____

FAVORITE/WANTED   NEEDED

NAME:

SHIRT SIZE: _____ PANTS SIZE: _____ SHOE SIZE: _____

FAVORITE/WANTED   NEEDED

NAME:

SHIRT SIZE: _____ PANTS SIZE: _____ SHOE SIZE: _____

FAVORITE/WANTED   NEEDED

NAME:

SHIRT SIZE: _____ PANTS SIZE: _____ SHOE SIZE: _____

FAVORITE/WANTED   NEEDED

NAME:

SHIRT SIZE: _____ PANTS SIZE: _____ SHOE SIZE: _____

FAVORITE/WANTED   NEEDED

NAME:

SHIRT SIZE: _____ PANTS SIZE: _____ SHOE SIZE: _____

FAVORITE/WANTED   NEEDED

NAME:_____

SHIRT SIZE:_____ PANTS SIZE:_____ SHOE SIZE:_____

FAVORITE/WANTED

NEEDED

NAME:_____

SHIRT SIZE:_____ PANTS SIZE:_____ SHOE SIZE:_____

FAVORITE/WANTED

NEEDED

NAME:_____

SHIRT SIZE:_____ PANTS SIZE:_____ SHOE SIZE:_____

FAVORITE/WANTED

NEEDED

NAME:_____

SHIRT SIZE:_____ PANTS SIZE:_____ SHOE SIZE:_____

FAVORITE/WANTED

NEEDED

NAME:_____

SHIRT SIZE:_____ PANTS SIZE:_____ SHOE SIZE:_____

FAVORITE/WANTED

NEEDED

NAME:_____

SHIRT SIZE:_____ PANTS SIZE:_____ SHOE SIZE:_____

FAVORITE/WANTED

NEEDED

NAME:_____

SHIRT SIZE:_____ PANTS SIZE:_____ SHOE SIZE:_____

FAVORITE/WANTED

NEEDED

NAME:_____

SHIRT SIZE:_____ PANTS SIZE:_____ SHOE SIZE:_____

FAVORITE/WANTED

NEEDED

NAME:_____

SHIRT SIZE:_____ PANTS SIZE:_____ SHOE SIZE:_____

FAVORITE/WANTED

NEEDED

NAME:_____

SHIRT SIZE:_____ PANTS SIZE:_____ SHOE SIZE:_____

FAVORITE/WANTED

NEEDED

TIP DON'T FORGET TO MAKE A LIST FOR YOURSELF! WHAT WOULD YOU LOVE TO GET FOR CHRISTMAS THIS YEAR?

CHRISTMAS GIFT LIST

FOUND THE PERFECT PRESENT? JOT IT DOWN HERE TO KEEP YOURSELF ORGANIZED.

NAME	GIFT	PRICE	WRAPPED

CHRISTMAS GIFT TAGS

PHOTOCOPY OR CUT OUT AND USE THESE GIFT TAGS FOR YOUR CHRISTMAS GIFTS.

CHRISTMAS CARD LIST

WHETHER YOU SEND A SIMPLE CHRISTMAS CARD WITH A PHOTO OR TYPE UP A FAMILY NEWSLETTER, KEEP TRACK OF WHO YOU NEED TO SEND A LITTLE HOLIDAY LOVE TO.

NAME	ADDRESS	MAILED
		☐
		☐
		☐
		☐
		☐
		☐
		☐
		☐
		☐
		☐
		☐
		☐
		☐
		☐
		☐
		☐
		☐
		☐
		☐
		☐
		☐
		☐
		☐
		☐

Deck the
HALLS

❄

GUEST LIST & CONTACT INFO

NAME _____   PHONE NUMBER _____   RSVP   ATTENDING?
ADDRESS _____   EMAIL ADDRESS _____   ☐   ☐

NAME _____   PHONE NUMBER _____   RSVP   ATTENDING?
ADDRESS _____   EMAIL ADDRESS _____   ☐   ☐

NAME _____   PHONE NUMBER _____   RSVP   ATTENDING?
ADDRESS _____   EMAIL ADDRESS _____   ☐   ☐

NAME _____   PHONE NUMBER _____   RSVP   ATTENDING?
ADDRESS _____   EMAIL ADDRESS _____   ☐   ☐

NAME _____   PHONE NUMBER _____   RSVP   ATTENDING?
ADDRESS _____   EMAIL ADDRESS _____   ☐   ☐

NAME _____   PHONE NUMBER _____   RSVP   ATTENDING?
ADDRESS _____   EMAIL ADDRESS _____   ☐   ☐

NAME _____   PHONE NUMBER _____   RSVP   ATTENDING?
ADDRESS _____   EMAIL ADDRESS _____   ☐   ☐

NAME _____   PHONE NUMBER _____   RSVP   ATTENDING?
ADDRESS _____   EMAIL ADDRESS _____   ☐   ☐

NAME _____   PHONE NUMBER _____   RSVP   ATTENDING?
ADDRESS _____   ADDRESS _____   ☐   ☐

NAME _____   PHONE NUMBER _____   RSVP   ATTENDING?
ADDRESS _____   EMAIL ADDRESS _____   ☐   ☐

NAME _____   PHONE NUMBER _____   RSVP   ATTENDING?
ADDRESS _____   EMAIL ADDRESS _____   ☐   ☐

NAME _____   PHONE NUMBER _____   RSVP   ATTENDING?
ADDRESS _____   EMAIL ADDRESS _____   ☐   ☐

NAME _____   PHONE NUMBER _____   RSVP   ATTENDING?
ADDRESS _____   EMAIL ADDRESS _____   ☐   ☐

CHRISTMAS

PARTY PLANNING COUNTDOWN

DECK THE HALLS AND GET READY FOR A CHRISTMAS PARTY YOU'LL NEVER FORGET!

3-4 WEEKS BEFORE

- [ ] PLAN THE MENU
- [ ] CREATE GROCERY LIST
- [ ] CREATE GUEST LIST
- [ ] DISPENSE FOOD ASSIGNMENTS
- [ ] DESIGN INVITATIONS (OPTIONAL)
- [ ] INVENTORY COOKING EQUIPMENT
- [ ] ARRANGE TO BORROW ANY NEEDED SUPPLIES
- [ ] PLAN DECORATIONS (TABLE, HOME, AND SO ON)
- [ ] BUY ANY NECESSARY DECORATIONS
- [ ] DECORATE NOW OR A LITTLE LATER

2 WEEKS BEFORE

- [ ] MAP OUT THE BEST PLACES TO BUY FOOD
- [ ] CLIP COUPONS AND COMPARE PRICES
- [ ] BUY THE TURKEY AND NONPERISHABLE FOOD TO AVOID THE RUSH
- [ ] BUY DECORATIONS
- [ ] SEND OUT INVITATIONS IF NECESSARY
- [ ] CONFIRM FOOD ASSIGNMENTS WITH FAMILY

1 WEEK BEFORE

- [ ] GATHER ENOUGH TABLES AND CHAIRS
- [ ] BEGIN CLEANING THE HOUSE (START WITH LOWER-TRAFFIC AREAS)
- [ ] BUY ANY NEEDED BULK ITEMS (SUCH AS PAPER PLATES, PLASTIC WARE, AND SO ON)
- [ ] CONFIRM WITH GUESTS THAT THEY'RE ATTENDING

- [ ] TRY OUT ANY NEW RECIPES TO MAKE SURE YOU WANT TO SERVE THEM
- [ ] GATHER TABLECLOTHS IF NEEDED

WEEK OF

- [ ] BUY PERISHABLE FOOD ITEMS
- [ ] CONFIRM WITH ANY GUESTS WHO HAVEN'T RESPONDED TO THE INVITATION
- [ ] DOUBLE-CHECK FOOD ASSIGNMENTS
- [ ] CLEAN HIGHER-TRAFFIC AREAS (BATHROOMS, BEDROOMS, LIVING ROOM, KITCHEN)
- [ ] BRINE TURKEY IF NECESSARY
- [ ] GATHER SERVING DISHES, SILVERWARE, AND SO ON
- [ ] WASH THE LINENS

DAY BEFORE

- [ ] MAKE THE PIES AND OTHER GOODIES
- [ ] PREPARE ANY "MAKE-AHEAD" RECIPES
- [ ] CLEAN ANY REMAINING AREAS/ROOMS
- [ ] VACUUM
- [ ] PUT ANY FINISHING TOUCHES ON THE TABLE DECORATIONS

DAY OF

- [ ] SET THE TABLE
- [ ] PUT THE FOOD IN THE OVEN ON TIME
- [ ] COOK ANY DISHES ASSIGNED TO YOU— DON'T FORGET THOSE EXTRAS
- [ ] WELCOME GUESTS
- [ ] ENJOY YOUR MEAL!

PARTY PLANNING

PARTY DATE: _____   PARTY BEGINS: _____   PARTY ENDS: _____

PARTY THEME: _____

PARTY STYLE: _____

THEME IDEAS

- SANTA'S WORKSHOP—ASK GUESTS TO BRING A TOY OR PRESENT TO DONATE TO A SUB-FOR-SANTA OR OTHER CHARITY

- WINTER WONDERLAND—DECORATE BY USING WHITE, SILVER, SHADES OF BLUE, AND SNOWFLAKES

- ALOHA CHRISTMAS—HOST A HAWAIIAN LUAU COMPLETE WITH LEIS, TROPICAL FOODS, PALM TREES, AND HAWAIIAN BARBECUE

ACTIVITIES

_____

_____

_____

_____

_____

TIP INCLUDE A CHRISTMAS COOKIE EXCHANGE AT YOUR PARTY. THEY ARE ALWAYS A HIT!

Under the
MISTLETOE

CHRISTMAS MENU PLAN

WHAT'S ON THE MENU? PLANNING IT OUT IN ADVANCE WILL HELP YOU KEEP TRACK OF
ALL THE DELICIOUS FOODS THAT WILL BE PART OF YOUR HOLIDAY CELEBRATION!

MEAL LOCATION: _____

TIME AND DATE: _____

	COURSE/MENU ITEM	RECIPE SOURCE	WHO'S MAKING IT?
APPETIZER			
APPETIZER			
APPETIZER			
APPETIZER			
SALAD			
BREAD			
ENTREE			
ENTREE			
MAIN DISH			
MAIN DISH			
SIDE DISH			
SIDE DISH			
DESSERT			
DESSERT			
BEVERAGES			
OTHER			
OTHER			
OTHER			
OTHER			

TIP CHECK WITH YOUR GUESTS TO SEE IF THERE ARE ANY
FOOD ALLERGIES OR DIETARY RESTRICTIONS YOU SHOULD
BE AWARE OF WHEN PLANNING YOUR MEAL.

THINGS TO MAKE & THINGS TO BUY

NOT EVERYTHING NEEDS TO BE HOMEMADE TO MAKE A MEMORABLE GOURMET MEAL. TAKE SOME
OF THE STRESS OFF AND USE SOME THINGS PREMADE FROM THE STORE. KEEP TRACK OF WHAT
FOODS YOU'LL BE MAKING AND WHAT FOODS YOU'LL BE BUYING.

THINGS TO MAKE	THINGS TO BUY

TIP IF THERE WILL BE YOUNGER KIDS AT YOUR CHRISTMAS DINNER OR
BREAKFAST, MAKE SURE THERE ARE PLENTY OF KID-FRIENDLY FOODS
AVAILABLE AND A KIDS' TABLE SET UP JUST FOR THEM.

GROCERY LIST

MAKE A LIST OF EVERYTHING YOU'LL NEED SO YOU WON'T HAVE TO MAKE ANY LAST-MINUTE TRIPS TO THE STORE.

PRODUCE
- [ ]
- [ ]
- [ ]
- [ ]
- [ ]
- [ ]

MEAT/POULTRY
- [ ]
- [ ]
- [ ]
- [ ]
- [ ]
- [ ]

DELI/BAKERY
- [ ]
- [ ]
- [ ]
- [ ]
- [ ]
- [ ]

CANNED GOODS
- [ ]
- [ ]
- [ ]
- [ ]
- [ ]
- [ ]

DRY GOODS
- [ ]
- [ ]
- [ ]
- [ ]
- [ ]
- [ ]

BAKING ITEMS/SPICES
- [ ]
- [ ]
- [ ]
- [ ]
- [ ]
- [ ]

CONDIMENTS
- [ ]
- [ ]
- [ ]
- [ ]
- [ ]
- [ ]

SNACKS
- [ ]
- [ ]
- [ ]
- [ ]
- [ ]
- [ ]

DAIRY
- [ ]
- [ ]
- [ ]
- [ ]
- [ ]
- [ ]

DRINKS
- [ ]
- [ ]
- [ ]
- [ ]
- [ ]
- [ ]

FROZEN
- [ ]
- [ ]
- [ ]
- [ ]
- [ ]
- [ ]

MISCELLANEOUS
- [ ]
- [ ]
- [ ]
- [ ]
- [ ]
- [ ]

COOKING SCHEDULE

WHETHER IT'S A QUIET CHRISTMAS EVE DINNER OR A BUSY BREAKFAST OR BRUNCH ON CHRISTMAS DAY, PLANNING OUT YOUR CHRISTMAS MENU WILL HELP YOU STAY ON TASK, WHISK AWAY THE STRESS, AND CREATE SOMETHING DELICIOUS!

DISH	WEEK OF	DAY BEFORE	DAY OF	COOKING METHOD	COOKING/SERVING DISH	PREP TIME	BAKING/ COOKING TIME	COOKING TEMP

DAY BEFORE

6 AM					
7 AM					
8 AM					
9 AM					
10 AM					
11 AM					
12 PM					
1 PM					
2 PM					
3 PM					
4 PM					
5 PM					
6 PM					
7 PM					

DAY OF

6 AM					
7 AM					
8 AM					
9 AM					
10 AM					
11 AM					
12 PM					
1 PM					
2 PM					
3 PM					
4 PM					
5 PM					
6 PM					
7 PM					

PREP LIST ORDER

65

Let it
SNOW

❄

CHRISTMAS BAKING PLANNER

PLANNING ON BAKING HOMEMADE GIFTS FOR NEIGHBORS THIS YEAR? OR ARE YOU MAKING BATCHES OF TREATS FOR FAMILY GATHERINGS? KEEP TRACK OF IT ALL HERE.

ITEM	# OF BATCHES TO MAKE	RECIPE SOURCE	MAKE FOR (PEOPLE/ EVENT/DATE)	MADE	SENT

RECIPES

BAKED HAM

1 (12-lb.) bone-in ham, rump portion
½ cup whole cloves
1 cup packed brown sugar

¼ cup garlic powder
4 cups water, or as needed

1. Preheat the oven to 350 degrees F (175 degrees C).

2. Place ham in a roasting pan, pierce top with a sharp knife all over surface and press whole cloves into the top at 1 to 2 inch intervals. Combine brown sugar and garlic powder. Pack the top of the ham with a layer of brown sugar mixture. Fill roasting pan with 1 inch of water. Cover the pan tightly with aluminum foil or a lid.

3. Bake for 4½ to 5 hours in the preheated oven (about 22 minutes per pound) or until the internal temperature of the ham has reached 160 degrees F (72 degrees C). Make sure the meat thermometer is not touching the bone. Let rest for 20 minutes before carving.

SCALLOPED POTATOES

1½ pounds red potatoes
   (about 12), thinly sliced
2 tablespoons butter,
   cubed and divided
1 pint half-and-half

2 tsp. garlic powder
salt and pepper to taste
2½ cups shredded Cheddar cheese
   or cheese of your choice, divided
1 Tbsp. chives, optional

1. Preheat the oven to 325 degrees F (165 degrees C). Grease a 1½ quart or larger baking dish with nonstick cooking spray.

2. Layer half of the potato slices in the bottom of baking dish. Reserve ½ cup cheese. Dot potatoes intermittently with 1 tablespoon of butter. Pour one-half pint of half-and-half over the top. Sprinkle with garlic powder then one cup of cheese. Season with salt and pepper. Repeat layering with remaining ingredients.

3. Bake for 30 minutes. Sprinkle remaining ½ cup cheese on top and bake for 30 minutes until potatoes are tender. Garnish with chopped chives if desired.

CHRISTMAS MORNING HAM STRATA

12 slices white bread,
   crusts removed
1½ cups grated cheddar cheese
1 cup cubed ham
4 eggs

3 cups whole milk
½ tsp. Worcestershire sauce
½ tsp. dry mustard
½ tsp. salt

1. Butter six slices of bread and place butter-side down in a greased 9x13-inch baking pan. Sprinkle ham and cheese evenly on top.

2. Butter remaining six slices of bread and place them on top, butter-side up.

3. Beat together eggs, milk, and seasonings.

4. Pour mixture over the top of the bread and then refrigerate for several hours (overnight is best).

5. Bake at 325 degrees F (165 degrees C) for one hour.

SOFT SUGAR COOKIES

½ cup shortening
1 cup sugar
1 egg, unbeaten
1 tsp. vanilla

½ cup sour milk (put 2 tsp.
   vinegar in milk to sour)
3¼ cups flour
2 tsp. baking soda
½ tsp. salt

1. Mix shortening, sugar, egg, and vanilla and beat for two minutes. Add sour milk and blend.

2. Mix together flour, baking soda, and salt and add to mixture.

3. Roll dough ¼-inch thick and cut into shapes

4. Bake at 425 degrees F (220 degrees C) for 10 minutes.

TIP: Don't add too much flour when rolling out and do not overbake.

NOW IT'S YOUR TURN! WRITE DOWN YOUR TRADITIONAL
CHRISTMAS RECIPES FOR EASY ACCESS.

Jingle all
THE WAY

TRADITIONS

TAKE TIME TO REFLECT ON SOME OF YOUR FAVORITE
CHRISTMAS EVE OR CHRISTMAS DAY FAMILY TRADITIONS.

TRADITION: _____

_____
_____
_____
_____
_____

TRADITION: _____

_____
_____
_____
_____
_____

TRADITION: _____

_____
_____
_____
_____
_____

DO YOU HAVE ANY CHRISTMAS TRADITIONS THAT ARE UNIQUE TO YOUR FAMILY?

TRADITION: _____

_____

_____

_____

_____

_____

TRADITION: _____

_____

_____

_____

_____

_____

TRADITION: _____

_____

_____

_____

_____

_____

WHAT TRADITIONS WOULD YOU LIKE TO START NEXT CHRISTMAS?

NEW TRADITION: _____

_____

_____

_____

_____

_____

NEW TRADITION: _____

_____

_____

_____

_____

_____

NEW TRADITION: _____

_____

_____

_____

_____

_____

Home for
THE HOLIDAYS

REFLECTIONS

WHAT ARE SOME OF YOUR FAVORITE CHRISTMAS EVE AND
CHRISTMAS MEMORIES THIS YEAR?

MEMORY: _____

_____

_____

_____

_____

_____

MEMORY: _____

_____

_____

_____

_____

_____

MEMORY: _____

_____

_____

_____

_____

_____

WHAT WAS YOUR FAVORITE GIFT YOU GAVE SOMEONE?

WHAT WAS YOUR FAVORITE GIFT YOU RECEIVED?

WHAT FAMILY AND FRIENDS DID YOU GET TO SPEND TIME WITH OR KEEP IN TOUCH WITH THIS CHRISTMAS?

WHAT DO YOU LOOK FORWARD TO NEXT CHRISTMAS?

USE THE SPACE BELOW FOR ANY OTHER THOUGHTS OR MEMORIES.

Season's
GREETINGS

THANK YOU NOTE LIST

DON'T FORGET TO SEND THOSE THANK-YOU NOTES! SHARE THE HOLIDAY LOVE
AND LET YOUR FRIENDS AND FAMILY KNOW YOU'RE GRATEFUL
FOR ALL THE WONDERFUL GIFTS YOU RECEIVED.

GIVER	GIFT RECEIVED	ADDRESS	MAILED
			☐
			☐
			☐
			☐
			☐
			☐
			☐
			☐
			☐
			☐
			☐
			☐
			☐
			☐
			☐
			☐
			☐
			☐
			☐
			☐
			☐

{ PHOTO }

{PHOTO}

{PHOTO}

{PHOTO}

{PHOTO}

{PHOTO}

JANUARY

"IN THE NEW YEAR, MAY YOUR
RIGHT HAND ALWAYS BE
STRETCHED OUT IN FRIENDSHIP,
BUT NEVER IN WANT."
    —IRISH TOAST

JANUARY

SUNDAY	MONDAY	TUESDAY

WEDNESDAY	THURSDAY	FRIDAY	SATURDAY

Cheers for a
HAPPY NEW YEAR

TO-DO LIST

JOT DOWN ALL THE THINGS YOU NEED TO DO TO GET READY FOR YOUR
NEW YEAR'S EVE BASH AND CHECK THEM OFF AS YOU GO!

- [ ] _____
- [ ] _____
- [ ] _____
- [ ] _____
- [ ] _____
- [ ] _____
- [ ] _____
- [ ] _____
- [ ] _____
- [ ] _____
- [ ] _____
- [ ] _____
- [ ] _____
- [ ] _____

- [ ] _____
- [ ] _____
- [ ] _____
- [ ] _____
- [ ] _____
- [ ] _____
- [ ] _____
- [ ] _____
- [ ] _____
- [ ] _____
- [ ] _____
- [ ] _____
- [ ] _____
- [ ] _____

NEW YEAR'S BUDGET

PLAN AHEAD FOR ALL YOUR NEW YEAR'S EVE EXPENSES

	ESTIMATED	ACTUAL
GREETINGS	$	$
PHOTOS		
CARDS		
ENVELOPES		
POSTAGE		
INVITATIONS		
DECOR	$	$
PARTY HATS		
NOISEMAKERS		
BALLOONS		
INDOOR DECORATIONS		
OUTDOOR DECORATIONS		
SUPPLIES		
CRAFT SUPPLIES		
OTHER		
OTHER		

	ESTIMATED	ACTUAL
FOOD	$	$
HOLIDAY MEALS		
PARTIES		
BAKING		
EATING OUT		
DRINKS		
OTHER		
TRAVEL	$	$
TRANSPORTATION		
LODGING		
OTHER		
MISCELLANEOUS	$	$
CLOTHING		
TICKETS		

	ESTIMATED	ACTUAL
TOTALS	$	$

NEW YEAR'S DECORATIONS

KEEP TRACK OF ALL YOUR NEW YEAR'S DECORATION IDEAS

DECORATION	HAVE	NEED	WHERE TO BUY/BORROW

SUPPLIES	HAVE	NEED	WHERE TO BUY/BORROW

See you at

MIDNIGHT

GUEST LIST & CONTACT INFO

NAME _____ PHONE NUMBER _____ RSVP ATTENDING?
ADDRESS _____ EMAIL ADDRESS _____ ☐   ☐

NAME _____ PHONE NUMBER _____ RSVP ATTENDING?
ADDRESS _____ EMAIL ADDRESS _____ ☐   ☐

NAME _____ PHONE NUMBER _____ RSVP ATTENDING?
ADDRESS _____ EMAIL ADDRESS _____ ☐   ☐

NAME _____ PHONE NUMBER _____ RSVP ATTENDING?
ADDRESS _____ EMAIL ADDRESS _____ ☐   ☐

NAME _____ PHONE NUMBER _____ RSVP ATTENDING?
ADDRESS _____ EMAIL ADDRESS _____ ☐   ☐

NAME _____ PHONE NUMBER _____ RSVP ATTENDING?
ADDRESS _____ EMAIL ADDRESS _____ ☐   ☐

NAME _____ PHONE NUMBER _____ RSVP ATTENDING?
ADDRESS _____ EMAIL ADDRESS _____ ☐   ☐

NAME _____ PHONE NUMBER _____ RSVP ATTENDING?
ADDRESS _____ EMAIL ADDRESS _____ ☐   ☐

NAME _____ PHONE NUMBER _____ RSVP ATTENDING?
ADDRESS _____ EMAIL ADDRESS _____ ☐   ☐

NAME _____ PHONE NUMBER _____ RSVP ATTENDING?
ADDRESS _____ EMAIL ADDRESS _____ ☐   ☐

NAME _____ PHONE NUMBER _____ RSVP ATTENDING?
ADDRESS _____ EMAIL ADDRESS _____ ☐   ☐

NAME _____ PHONE NUMBER _____ RSVP ATTENDING?
ADDRESS _____ EMAIL ADDRESS _____ ☐   ☐

NEW YEAR'S EVE

PARTY PLANNING COUNTDOWN

OUT WITH THE OLD, AND IN WITH THE AWESOME!

3-4 WEEKS BEFORE

- [ ] PLAN THE THEME
- [ ] PLAN THE MENU
- [ ] CREATE GROCERY LIST
- [ ] CREATE GUEST LIST
- [ ] DISPENSE FOOD ASSIGNMENTS
- [ ] INVENTORY COOKING EQUIPMENT
- [ ] ARRANGE TO BORROW ANY NEEDED SUPPLIES
- [ ] INVENTORY DECORATIONS
- [ ] PLAN DECORATIONS (TABLE, HOME, AND SO ON)
- [ ] BUY ANY NECESSARY DECORATIONS
- [ ] DECORATE YOUR HOME NOW OR LATER

2 WEEKS BEFORE

- [ ] MAP OUT THE BEST PLACES TO BUY FOOD IF YOU'RE PLANNING A LARGE PARTY
- [ ] CLIP COUPONS AND COMPARE PRICES
- [ ] BUY NONPERISHABLE FOODS (TO AVOID THE RUSH)
- [ ] SEND OUT INVITATIONS
- [ ] PLAN PARTY GAMES
- [ ] MAKE FOOD ASSIGNMENTS
- [ ] ARRANGE FOR A BABYSITTER IF YOU'RE PLANNING AN ADULT PARTY

1 WEEK BEFORE

- [ ] GATHER ENOUGH CHAIRS
- [ ] BEGIN CLEANING THE HOUSE (START WITH LOWER-TRAFFIC AREAS)
- [ ] BUY ANY NEEDED BULK ITEMS (SUCH AS PAPER PLATES, PLASTICWARE, AND SO ON)
- [ ] CONFIRM WITH GUESTS THAT THEY'RE ATTENDING
- [ ] BUY PARTY FAVORS

WEEK OF

- [ ] BUY PERISHABLE FOOD ITEMS
- [ ] CONFIRM WITH ANY GUESTS WHO HAVEN'T RESPONDED TO THE INVITATION
- [ ] CLEAN HIGHER-TRAFFIC AREAS (BATHROOMS, BEDROOMS, LIVING ROOM, KITCHEN)
- [ ] GATHER SERVING DISHES, SILVERWARE, AND SO ON
- [ ] CONFIRM FOOD ASSIGNMENTS

DAY BEFORE

- [ ] CLEAN ANY REMAINING AREAS/ROOMS
- [ ] VACUUM
- [ ] PUT ANY FINISHING TOUCHES ON THE DECORATIONS
- [ ] PREPARE ANY MAKE-AHEAD FOOD ITEMS

DAY OF

- [ ] PREPARE ANY REMAINING FOOD ITEMS
- [ ] STRAIGHTEN ANY REMAINING AREAS

NIGHT OF

- [ ] ENJOY YOUR PARTY!

TIP MAKE SURE TO HAVE A WAY TO WATCH THE BALL DROP AT MIDNIGHT (VIA INTERNET, CABLE, SATELLITE, AND SO ON).

PARTY PLANNING

PARTY DATE: _____ PARTY BEGINS: _____ PARTY ENDS: _____

PARTY THEME: _____

PARTY STYLE: _____

THEME IDEAS

- BLAST FROM THE PAST—GUESTS WEAR THE CLOTHES OF PREVIOUS DECADES: 1920S, 1950S, 1970S, AND 1980S ARE ALL REALLY FUN.

- A BLACK-TIE AFFAIR—GUESTS WEAR THEIR BEST FORMAL ATTIRE.

- RED CARPET STARS—GUESTS DRESS AS THEIR FAVORITE CELEBRITIES.

- NEW YEAR, NEW YOU!—SERVE ONLY HEALTHY MENU OPTIONS.

ACTIVITIES

_____

_____

_____

_____

_____

TIP CREATIVE HORS D'OEUVRES ARE ALWAYS A HIT AT NEW YEAR'S PARTIES.

It's time to
CELEBRATE

NEW YEAR'S MENU PLAN

WHAT'S ON THE MENU? PLANNING IT OUT IN ADVANCE WILL HELP YOU KEEP TRACK OF
ALL THE DELICIOUS FOODS THAT WILL BE PART OF YOUR HOLIDAY CELEBRATION!

MEAL LOCATION: _____

TIME AND DATE: _____

	COURSE/MENU ITEM	RECIPE SOURCE	WHO'S MAKING IT?
APPETIZER			
APPETIZER			
APPETIZER			
APPETIZER			
APPETIZER			
APPETIZER			
SALAD			
BREAD			
ENTREE			
ENTREE			
MAIN DISH			
MAIN DISH			
SIDE DISH			
SIDE DISH			
DESSERT			
DESSERT			
BEVERAGES			
OTHER			
OTHER			

TIP CHECK WITH YOUR GUESTS TO SEE IF THERE ARE ANY
FOOD ALLERGIES OR DIETARY RESTRICTIONS YOU SHOULD
BE AWARE OF WHEN PLANNING YOUR MEAL.

THINGS TO MAKE & THINGS TO BUY

NOT EVERYTHING NEEDS TO BE HOMEMADE TO MAKE A MEMORABLE GOURMET MEAL. TAKE SOME OF THE STRESS OFF AND USE SOME THINGS PREMADE FROM THE STORE. KEEP TRACK OF WHAT FOODS YOU'LL BE MAKING AND WHAT FOODS YOU'LL BE BUYING.

THINGS TO MAKE	THINGS TO BUY

TIP IF THERE WILL BE YOUNGER KIDS AT YOUR NEW YEAR'S EVE BASH, MAKE SURE THERE ARE PLENTY OF KID-FRIENDLY FOODS AVAILABLE AND A KIDS' AREA SET UP JUST FOR THEM.

GROCERY LIST

MAKE A LIST OF EVERYTHING YOU'LL NEED SO YOU WON'T HAVE TO MAKE ANY LAST-MINUTE TRIPS TO THE STORE.

PRODUCE

- ☐ _____
- ☐ _____
- ☐ _____
- ☐ _____
- ☐ _____
- ☐ _____

MEAT/POULTRY

- ☐ _____
- ☐ _____
- ☐ _____
- ☐ _____
- ☐ _____
- ☐ _____

DELI/BAKERY

- ☐ _____
- ☐ _____
- ☐ _____
- ☐ _____
- ☐ _____
- ☐ _____

CANNED GOODS

- ☐ _____
- ☐ _____
- ☐ _____
- ☐ _____
- ☐ _____
- ☐ _____

DRY GOODS

- ☐ _____
- ☐ _____
- ☐ _____
- ☐ _____
- ☐ _____
- ☐ _____

BAKING ITEMS/SPICES

- ☐ _____
- ☐ _____
- ☐ _____
- ☐ _____
- ☐ _____
- ☐ _____

CONDIMENTS

- ☐ _____
- ☐ _____
- ☐ _____
- ☐ _____
- ☐ _____
- ☐ _____

SNACKS

- ☐ _____
- ☐ _____
- ☐ _____
- ☐ _____
- ☐ _____
- ☐ _____

DAIRY

- ☐ _____
- ☐ _____
- ☐ _____
- ☐ _____
- ☐ _____

DRINKS

- ☐ _____
- ☐ _____
- ☐ _____
- ☐ _____
- ☐ _____
- ☐ _____

FROZEN

- ☐ _____
- ☐ _____
- ☐ _____
- ☐ _____
- ☐ _____
- ☐ _____

MISCELLANEOUS

- ☐ _____
- ☐ _____
- ☐ _____
- ☐ _____
- ☐ _____
- ☐ _____

COOKING SCHEDULE

HOSTING A NEW YEAR'S EVE SOIREE CAN FEEL LIKE AN OVERWHELMING TASK. BUT PLANNING YOUR MENU AND KEEPING TRACK OF ALL THE STEPS THAT NEED TO BE DONE WILL TAKE AWAY THE STRESS AND HELP YOU PREPARE THE PERFECT SPREAD!

DISH	WEEK OF	DAY BEFORE	DAY OF	COOKING METHOD	COOKING/SERVING DISH	PREP TIME	BAKING/ COOKING TIME	COOKING TEMP

DAY BEFORE

6 AM					
7 AM					
8 AM					
9 AM					
10 AM					
11 AM					
12 PM					
1 PM					
2 PM					
3 PM					
4 PM					
5 PM					
6 PM					
7 PM					

DAY OF

6 AM					
7 AM					
8 AM					
9 AM					
10 AM					
11 AM					
12 PM					
1 PM					
2 PM					
3 PM					
4 PM					
5 PM					
6 PM					
7 PM					

RECIPES

HERE ARE A FEW RECIPES TO HELP YOU CREATE DELICIOUS THINGS TO EAT WHILE YOU WAIT FOR THE BALL TO DROP!

EGGNOG

12 eggs
½ cup sugar
8 cups milk

2 tsp. vanilla extract
¼ tsp. nutmeg

1. Whisk the eggs and sugar in a bowl until light colored and frothy.

2. Transfer to a medium saucepan and whisk in 2 cups of milk until thoroughly blended.

3. Place the pan over medium heat and continue to stir until the mixture thickens and coats the back of a wooden spoon, about 5 minutes.

4. Remove from heat and allow to stand for 5 minutes.

5. Stir in the remaining 6 cups of milk, vanilla extract, and nutmeg. Refrigerate at least 2 hours to cool thoroughly before serving.

EASY CHEESE BALL

2 (8-oz.) pkgs. cream
  cheese, softened

1 (1-oz.) pkg.
  ranch dressing mix

¼ cup green onions,
  chopped (optional)

2 cups shredded cheddar cheese
  (or cheese of choice)

1½ cups chopped pecans

1. Mash cream cheese in a medium size bowl. Mix dressing, cheese, and onions into cream cheese.

2. Shape the mixture into a ball. Roll the ball in the chopped nuts.

3. Cover and refrigerate until ready to serve.

4. Serve with an assortment of crackers.

SPINACH ARTICHOKE DIP

2 (8-oz.) jars marinated artichoke hearts, drained and cut into pieces
1 (10-oz.) pkg. frozen spinach, thawed
½ cup mayonnaise
½ cup light sour cream
1 cups Italian style cheese
1 cup shredded Parmesan cheese
2 Tbsp. garlic powder
salt and pepper to taste

1. Preheat oven to 350 degrees F (177 degrees C). Thaw spinach and drain off any liquid.

2. Cut artichoke hearts into bite-size pieces.

3. Combine all the ingredients and mix well.

4. Pour into a greased casserole dish and sprinkle with extra cheese. Bake for 20–25 minutes or until golden brown and bubbly. Let cool.

5. Serve with crackers or cubed French bread.

APPLE NACHOS

5 large tart apples, sliced thin
2 Tbsp. lemon juice
2 cups chocolate chips
caramel sauce (ice cream topping)
½ tsp. salt, or less if desired
chopped nuts of your choice, optional

1. Spread apple slices on a platter, sprinkle with lemon juice, and set aside.

2. In the microwave, melt chocolate chips in 20-second increments on high, stirring between each increment. Keep in mind that chocolate chips can burn if heated too long.

3. Drizzle melted chocolate and caramel sauce over apple slices. Sprinkle salt over apple slices.

4. Refrigerate until ready to serve.

NOW IT'S YOUR TURN! WRITE DOWN YOUR TRADITIONAL
NEW YEAR'S RECIPES FOR EASY ACCESS.

Happy
NEW YEAR

TRADITIONS

TAKE TIME TO REFLECT ON SOME OF YOUR FAVORITE NEW YEAR'S EVE OR NEW YEAR'S DAY FAMILY TRADITIONS.

TRADITION: _____

_____

_____

_____

_____

_____

TRADITION: _____

_____

_____

_____

_____

_____

TRADITION: _____

_____

_____

_____

_____

_____

DO YOU HAVE ANY NEW YEAR'S TRADITIONS THAT ARE UNIQUE TO YOUR FAMILY?

TRADITION: _____

_____

_____

_____

_____

_____

TRADITION: _____

_____

_____

_____

_____

_____

TRADITION: _____

_____

_____

_____

_____

_____

WHAT NEW YEAR'S TRADITIONS WOULD YOU LIKE TO START NEXT YEAR?

NEW TRADITION:_____

_____

_____

_____

_____

_____

NEW TRADITION:_____

_____

_____

_____

_____

_____

NEW TRADITION:_____

_____

_____

_____

_____

_____

3...2...1...

HAPPY NEW YEAR!

REFLECTIONS

WHAT ARE SOME OF YOUR FAVORITE
NEW YEAR'S EVE MEMORIES THIS YEAR?

MEMORY: _____

_____

_____

_____

_____

_____

MEMORY: _____

_____

_____

_____

_____

_____

MEMORY: _____

_____

_____

_____

_____

WHAT WAS YOUR FAVORITE THING ABOUT THIS NEW YEAR'S EVE?

DID YOU GET A NEW YEAR'S EVE KISS AT MIDNIGHT? DETAILS?

WHAT FAMILY AND FRIENDS DID YOU GET TO SPEND TIME WITH OR KEEP IN TOUCH WITH TO BEGIN THE NEW YEAR?

WHAT DO YOU LOOK FORWARD TO IN THE NEW YEAR?

USE THE SPACE BELOW FOR ANY OTHER THOUGHTS OR MEMORIES.

Ring in the
NEW YEAR

GOALS FOR THE YEAR

SET GOALS FOR THE NEW YEAR AND KEEP TRACK OF
WHAT YOU NEED TO DO TO ACHIEVE THEM

FOR MY FAMILY

_____

_____

_____

**STEPS NEEDED TO
REACH MY GOAL**

1 _____
2 _____
3 _____
4 _____

ACCOMPLISH BY

_____

☐ DONE!

FOR MYSELF

_____

_____

_____

**STEPS NEEDED TO
REACH MY GOAL**

1 _____
2 _____
3 _____
4 _____

ACCOMPLISH BY

_____

☐ DONE!

FOR MY HEALTH

_____

_____

_____

**STEPS NEEDED TO
REACH MY GOAL**

1 _____
2 _____
3 _____
4 _____

ACCOMPLISH BY

_____

☐ DONE!

FOR MY CAREER

_____

_____

_____

**STEPS NEEDED TO
REACH MY GOAL**

1 _____
2 _____
3 _____
4 _____

ACCOMPLISH BY

_____

☐ DONE!

FOR MY FINANCES

_____

_____

_____

**STEPS NEEDED TO
REACH MY GOAL**

1 _____
2 _____
3 _____
4 _____

ACCOMPLISH BY

_____

☐ DONE!

{PHOTO}

{PHOTO}

{PHOTO}

{PHOTO}

{PHOTO}

{ PHOTO }

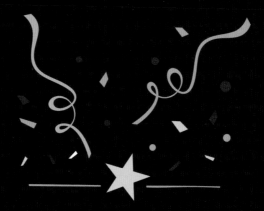

Celebrate a
NEW BEGINNING

• • • • • • • • • • • • • • • • • • • •

LETTER TO YOURSELF

REFLECT BACK ON THIS PAST YEAR AND WRITE A LETTER
TO YOURSELF IN THE SPACE BELOW:

DEAR _____ ,

_____

_____

_____

_____

_____

_____

_____

_____

_____

_____

_____

_____

_____

_____

_____

_____

_____

WHAT A YEAR THIS WAS!

SOME THINGS I LOVED ABOUT THIS YEAR WERE

_____

_____

_____

_____

MY FAVORITE MEMORY OF THIS YEAR WAS

_____

_____

_____

_____

THE GREATEST LESSON I LEARNED THIS YEAR WAS

_____

_____

_____

THE HARDEST THING TO DEAL WITH THIS YEAR WAS

_____

_____

_____

_____

THE BEST THING THAT HAPPENED THIS YEAR WAS

_____

_____

_____

_____

LOOK AHEAD TO NEXT YEAR

THINGS I WANT TO DO THIS COMING YEAR:

_____

_____

_____

_____

_____

_____

THINGS I WANT TO BECOME BETTER AT THIS YEAR:

_____

_____

_____

_____

_____

_____

THINGS I'M LOOKING FORWARD TO THIS YEAR:

_____

_____

_____

_____

_____

_____

_____

TO-DO LIST
FOR NEXT YEAR'S HOLIDAY SEASON
JOT DOWN ALL THE THINGS YOU NEED TO DO TO GET READY
FOR NEXT YEAR AND CHECK THEM OFF AS YOU GO!

☐ _____

☐ _____

☐ _____

☐ _____

☐ _____

☐ _____

☐ _____

☐ _____

☐ _____

☐ _____

☐ _____

☐ _____

☐ BUY A NEW COPY OF *THE NO-STRESS HOLIDAY ORGANIZER!*

0 26575 14917 3